$5 Meals Cookb
Friendly Recipes
by Madson Web Publishing, LLC

Family Menu Planning Series

Introduction

Stretch that dollar in style without having to sacrifice your favorite meals. This book shows you how to eat healthy on a small budget, whether cooking at college, feeding a family or just trying to live frugally. It's a perfect cookbook for those with a limited budget. The cookbook is loaded with healthy recipes that take extremely little time to prepare and have very few ingredients that are relatively cheap. Most of the ingredients are typical items found in almost every kitchen; there are no exotic spices in the cookbook that you have to go searching for all over the town.

We can't calculate how much it will cost at your store to make these meals but we've included our favorite low-cost meals that cost us $5 or less.

Disclaimer and Terms of Use: Effort has been made to ensure that the information in this book is accurate and complete, however, the author and the publisher do not warrant the accuracy of the information, text and graphics contained within the book due to the rapidly changing nature of science, research, known and unknown facts and internet. The Author and the publisher do not hold any responsibility for errors, omissions or contrary interpretation of the subject matter herein. This book is presented solely for motivational and informational purposes only.

Table of Contents

Tips for Frugal Eating

It's important to try and learn some good financial practices to help save money. Leading a frugal lifestyle doesn't imply never spending money –it means spending money wisely so it lasts longer.

With the current economy, everyone is trying to save a dollar. Eating healthy does not mean that you have to spend a fortune. Frugal eating can be very healthy for you while studying.

Meat every day? Not a must! You don't have to eat meat at every meal. Try using lentils and beans in your main dish recipes. Meals made with beans are usually larger in volume which often translates to even more frugal eating. If your recipe contains meat, include some lentils to increase the volume and add healthy protein at the same time.

Purchase veggies and fruits in season to get the best deal possible. At the peak of the season, you're sure to get fantastic prices for pepper, apples, and corn on the cob. Buy in large quantities, cook some and store the rest in the freezer.

Move away from pricey processed foods by **making your own natural products** more delicious with spices and herbs. You can use curry, cilantro, and cumin in your dishes. Although it can be very challenging to find the best and healthy ways to cut down dinner costs, it can be fun it you take your time to brainstorm.

Avoid wasting food: Make use of all your leftovers. You can use leftovers for lunches, for the next dinner, or to create another recipe. For instance, use leftover meat and veggies with a few new ingredients to make an excellent casserole or soup. If you can't eat something you prepared right away, freeze it for later use.

Draw a budget: Make a reasonable budget for food, and always try to stay within the set budget. Set aside a few dollars or coins on a weekly basis for stocking your pantry on sale items.

FRUGAL BREAKFAST RECIPES

I usually find warm food cheaper than buying sugary cereal. Eggs are great; they keep you going and make an excellent combo with carbs to produce energy to keep you going.

Deviled Eggs

These deviled eggs have a creamy filling that couldn't be quicker and easier to make.

Total Time: 25 Minutes

Prep Time: 15 Minutes

Cook Time: 10 Minutes

Yield: 24 halves

Ingredients

12 large eggs

pinch of pepper

1/4 tsp. salt

2 tsp. Dijon mustard

4 tbsp. mayonnaise

Directions

Arrange eggs in a single layer in a large saucepan and cover with water and bring to a boil. Reduce heat and simmer for about 9 minutes. Fill large bowl halfway with water and ice and add the cooked eggs to cool.

Peel the cold eggs and cut each into two equal parts lengthwise. Remove the yolks and put in a bowl; using a fork, mash the yolks until very smooth. Add mustard, mayonnaise, salt and pepper and combine well.

Transfer the yolk mixture to a piping bag* that's fitted with a star or plain tip; pipe the yolk mixture into the empty egg whites and serve.

*Or use a Ziploc bag and cut the tip of a corner.

~Buy a carton of 18 count or 30 count eggs for $4 or less and you'll have enough for more than one meal.

Potato Omelet

You can serve this potato omelet as is or you can stretch it further by using it as a sandwich filing.

Servings: 3

Ingredients

6 eggs

1-1/3 Cups olive oil

1 large potato, scrubbed and finely sliced

1/2 onion, peeled & finely sliced

Directions

Heat olive oil over medium heat. Add onion and cook, stirring, for a few minutes or until onion is tender and golden brown. Add potatoes; cook, covered, until the potatoes are tender but not mushy.

Beat the eggs in a small bowl, add a pinch of salt. Pour the egg mixture into the potato mixture and stir gently to distribute the eggs well under the potato. Smooth the top and let cook for a few minutes or until set. Pop the entire mixture under a hot grill and let cook until the omelet is a bit puffy.

~You should be able to buy a 5 lb bag of potatoes for $5 or less and will have many meals worth. Store potatoes in a dry, dark place.

Breakfast Banana Fruit Smoothie

This smoothie provides a healthy and great way to start your day. It's packed with essential nutrients and it's very delicious. You can adjust honey to your taste.

Total Time: 10 Minutes

Prep Time: 10 Minutes

Cook Time: 0 Minutes

Servings: 4

Ingredients

1 tbsp. honey

3 bananas, sliced

1 Cup apple or orange juice

2 Cups ice

Directions

Combine honey, bananas, juice, and ice in a blender and blend until very smooth. Pour into serving glasses and enjoy!

~Go cheaper by buying frozen juice concentrate compared to already mixed in a plastic bottle.

Cheap Healthy Omelet

This is probably the best omelet in the whole world! It's cheap and super healthy.

Total Time: 40 Minutes

Prep Time: 15 Minutes

Cook Time: 25 Minutes

Servings: 2

Ingredients

4 eggs

2 tbsp. butter

7 button mushrooms, sliced

1/2 sliced onion

1/2 chopped red bell pepper

1/2 chopped green bell pepper

Directions

In a medium sized saucepan, melt butter over medium heat. Stir in mushrooms, onion, red bell pepper and green bell pepper. Cook the mixture for about 5 minutes or until tender.

Stir in eggs and continue cooking for at least 10 minutes or until firm.

~Buy whichever mushrooms are cheaper at the store or on sale. Portobello mushrooms would be great in place of button but may be more expensive.

Potato Pancakes

Total Time: 35 Minutes

Prep Time: 15 Minutes

Cook Time: 20 Minutes

Ingredients

1/4 Cup plain flour

2 Cups mashed potatoes with no milk added

1 Tablespoon butter

Pinch salt

Pinch of black pepper

Directions

In a bowl, combine butter, mashed potatoes and seasoning; let cool.

Add flour, a small amount at a time, combining well.

The dough should be just stiff and not too sticky. Roll the dough on a lightly floured work surface until is about 1/2 inch thick. Cut the rolled dough into about 8 to 10 pieces.

Make a batch and layer them with a greaseproof paper and freeze. Cook as needed in oil until golden and crisp on both sides. Serve with fried eggs.

One Pan Crepe

This pancake has an eggy-soft center and crusty and browned outside. It's easy to prepare and cheap too.

Total Time: 25 Minutes

Prep Time: 10 Minutes

Cook Time: 15 Minutes

Servings: 4

Ingredients

3 Tablespoons. butter

2/3 Cup milk

1 tsp. salt

2/3 Cup flour

4 eggs

Directions

Preheat your oven to 225°C/450°F. Coat a heavy 10-inch oven proof skillet with butter and set aside.

In a large bowl, beat the eggs, using a fork until well blended. Gradually beat in flour. Stir in milk and salt until well combined. Transfer the batter to hot skillet; bake in the oven for at least 15 minutes.

Lower the oven heat to about 350°F and continue baking for another 10 minutes.

Remove the pancake from oven and sprinkle with sugar or maple syrup.

~You can stock up on butter cubes when it's on sale and freeze.

Greek Yogurt Parfait

This kiwi and Greek Yogurt Parfait recipe is going to start off your day the right way! Although this recipe is inexpensive, its ingredients can help in boosting weight loss and may even play a great role in managing asthma and improve digestion.

Total Time: 5 Minutes

Prep Time: 5 Minutes

Cook Time: 0 Minutes

Servings: 1

Ingredients

1 apple, banana or kiwi*, sliced

1/2 tsp. honey

1-2 drops vanilla extract

1/2 cup Greek yogurt

sprinkle of nuts or granola

Directions

Combine yogurt and vanilla extract in a small bowl and mix to blend well.

In a serving glass, layer the vanilla extract mixture, honey and slices of kiwi.

Top with nuts or granola, if desired.

Use whatever fruit is on sale!

Breakfast Almond Butter

Make your own almond butter for breakfast on an as-needed basis for almost half the cost of store-bought almond butter. It's perfect when spread over your favorite bread for a fantastic breakfast.

Ingredients

2 Cups roasted almonds

1Tablespoon. canola or almond oil

1 Tablespoon. ground cinnamon

1/2 Tablespoon vanilla extract

Directions

Put almonds in a blender and blend until finely ground. Add all the remaining ingredients and continue blending until smooth and creamy.

Store in a container or jar.

~Usually buying oil in bulk is cheaper in the long run if you store in a cool, dark place.

FRUGAL SNACKS

Garlicky Roasted Red Pepper Dip

Total Time: 45 Minutes

Prep Time: 5 Minutes

Cook Time: 40 Minutes

Yields: 8 Servings

Ingredients

1/2 Cup low-fat sour cream

1 head garlic

1 tsp. olive oil

1/4 tsp. ground coriander

Pinch of cayenne pepper

1/2 tsp. cumin

1 red bell pepper

Salt and pepper

Assorted crackers and crudités

Directions

Preheat your oven to 400ºF. Cut the top off the head of garlic and place on a sheet of foil. Drizzle with oil and season with salt and pepper. Tightly wrap garlic and roast for about 40 minutes or until tender. Let cool.

Cook bell pepper under preheated broiler or over an open flame, turning with tongs frequently, until blackened. Let cool and peel skin off.

Take out seeds and insides of peppers and chop coarsely. Squeeze the garlic out of skins. Combine the garlic and pepper in a blender; add sour cream, coriander, and cumin; blend until very smooth. Season the dip with salt and pepper and store in fridge. Serve the dip with assorted crackers and vegetables.

~Buying garlic in bulk is cheaper than buying minced garlic in a jar.

Lemon-Sugar Grilled Pineapple

Total Time: 12 Minutes

Prep Time: 5 Minutes

Cook Time: 7 Minutes

Yields: 2 Servings

Ingredients

2 Tablespoon grated lemon zest

1 can pineapple slices

1/2 cup sugar

1 Tablespoon cinnamon

Directions

In a zip-lock bag, combine lemon zest, cinnamon and sugar. Rub the bag vigorously to combine the flavors.

Prepare charcoal fire and let burn to a gray ash. Set the grill 6 inches from the coal.

Place pineapple pieces in the zip-lock bag with lemon zest mixture and shake to coat. Transfer the coated pineapple to the hot grill and let cook, flipping frequently, for about 7 minutes or until caramelized and slightly tender. Let cool slightly before serving.

~Buy fresh pineapple when in season or use canned slices.

Avocado-and-Tomato Salsa Crostini

Total Time: 40 Minutes

Prep Time: 20 Minutes

Cook Time: 20 Minutes

Yields: 4 Servings

Ingredients

1 Cup diced tomato

1 large avocado, pitted, peeled and cubed

1 long, thin baguette

1/4 Cup olive oil

2 tbsp. lime juice

1/2 small onion, finely chopped

2 Tablespoon. chopped fresh cilantro

Salt and pepper

Directions

Preheat the oven to 400°F. Cut the bread into about 1/4-inch-thick slices and arrange the slices on a baking sheet in a single layer. each bread slice with olive oil and season with salt and pepper. Toast bread until golden brown. Let cool completely.

Combine chopped tomatoes, avocado, lime juice, onion and cilantro in a small bowl. Sprinkle with salt and pepper; gently mix to combine well.

Top each toasted bread slice with a spoonful of salsa.

~You can buy day old French bread for this recipe since you will be toasting it. This is often cheaper.

Stuffed Cheese Puffs

Total Time: 40 Minutes

Prep Time: 10 Minutes

Cook Time: 30 Minutes

Yields: 8 Servings

Ingredients

4 large eggs

1 Cup all-purpose flour

3 Tablespoons. unsalted butter

1/2 tsp. freshly ground pepper

3/4 tsp. salt

1/2 cup cheddar or combination of cheese, finely shredded

tuna salad, chicken salad or other fillings of your choice

Directions

Preheat the oven to 400°F. Spray two cookie sheets with cooking spray. Combine butter, a cup of water, salt and pepper in a saucepan. Bring to a boil over medium-high heat. Beat in flour until mixture forms a ball of dough.

Place the dough in a large bowl and beat in the eggs one at a time, with an electric mixer on high speed. Add cheese and beat until the mixture is smooth.

Drop scoops of the dough one inch apart on the coated cookie sheets and smoothen the tops with the back of a spoon. Bake the dough for about 30 minutes or until golden and puffed. Transfer to wire racks to cool completely. Slice off the top third, discarding the doughy centers. Fill with salad and replace the tops, if desired.

~It is cheaper to buy cheese in a block and shred it yourself.

Garlic Pita Chips

Total Time: 18 Minutes

Prep Time: 10 Minutes

Cook Time: 8 Minutes

Yield: 8 Servings

Ingredients

6 (6-inch) pitas, split

1 teaspoon onion powder

1 teaspoon garlic salt

1/2 Cup olive oil

Salt and pepper

Directions

Preheat the oven to 425°F. Blend together in a small glass or cup, onion powder, garlic salt, a pinch of salt and pepper and olive oil.

Brush the oil mixture on the sides of pitas; stack and cut the pitas into wedges. Arrange half of the wedges with the oil sides facing up on two baking sheets and bake for about 5 minutes or until golden. Repeat the same procedure with the remaining wedges.

~A snack that is much cheaper made homemade than buying packaged.

FRUGAL DINNER RECIPES

Chili-Lime Drumsticks

Total Time: 55 Minutes

Prep Time: 5 Minutes

Cook Time: 50 Minutes

Yields: 8 Servings

Ingredients

16 chicken drumsticks

1 teaspoon brown sugar

2 cloves garlic, chopped

1 Tablespoon chili powder

1/4 Cup fresh lime juice

4 Tablespoons butter, melted

Salt and pepper

Directions

Preheat the oven to 400°F. Rinse and pat dry the drumsticks before seasoning with salt and pepper. Arrange in a single layer on two baking sheets.

In a bowl, combine all the remaining ingredients and pour over the drumsticks and turn to coat well.

Bake or grill chicken turning halfway through cooking for 40-45 minutes or until no longer pink.

~Buy chicken on sale and use whatever chicken is on sale, such as drumsticks, thighs or chicken breasts.

Chicken and Onion Kabobs

Total Time: 40 Minutes

Prep Time: 15 Minutes

Marinate: 15 Minutes

Cook Time: 10 Minutes

Servings: 4

Ingredients

bottled or homemade barbecue sauce

1 tbsp. lemon juice

2 tbsp. Worcestershire sauce

3 skinless, boneless chicken breasts, cubed

1 tbsp. extra virgin olive oil, and more for brushing

1 1/2 onions, quartered, layers separated

Salt and pepper

Directions

In a bowl, toss together chicken with olive oil, lemon juice, and Worcestershire sauce. Let the chicken marinate several hours.

Skewer the marinated chicken cubes onto eight metal skewers with onions. Brush with oil and sprinkle with salt and pepper.

Grill or broil the kabobs turning often while cooking.

Serve with barbecue sauce, if desired.

~Add other vegetables to your kabobs such as pepper cubes or whole fresh mushrooms.

Shredded Pork

Total Time: 6 Hours 10 Minutes

Prep Time: 10 Minutes

Cook Time: 6 Hours

Yields: 8 Servings

Ingredients

1 3-lb. pork shoulder, boneless, trimmed of fat, and chopped

3 cloves garlic

1 large onion, quartered

1/2 tsp. dried oregano

1/2 tsp. ground cumin

1 tsp. chili powder

2 tsp. salt

Directions

Sprinkle boneless pork shoulder with oregano, cumin, chili powder, and salt and transfer to a slow cooker. Add garlic and onion and cook, covered, on low for about 6 hours or until meat is soft and falling apart. Shred and serve hot.

Lamb Kabobs with Yogurt Sauce

Total Time: 30 Minutes

Prep Time: 15 Minutes

Cook Time: 15 Minutes

Yields: 4 Servings

Ingredients

Yogurt Sauce:

1/2 Cup plain yogurt

1/2 Cup sour cream

1 teaspoon dried parsley

1/4 teaspoon cumin

1 clove garlic, minced

2 Tablespoons lime juice

Salt and pepper

Kabobs

2 pounds lean lamb, cut into 2-inch chunks

1 yellow bell pepper, stemmed, seeded, cut into small pieces

1 red bell pepper, stemmed, seeded, cut into small pieces

1 small eggplant, cubed

1 tsp. ground cumin

2 tbsp. olive oil, and extra for brushing

Salt and pepper

Directions

In a bowl, stir together lime juice, sour cream and yogurt until well combined. Add parsley, cumin, garlic, salt and pepper. Cover and chill.

Combine oil, cumin, lamb, salt and pepper and toss to mix well. Thread the coated lamb onto eight metal skewers, alternating with vegetables.

Brush with oil and season with salt and pepper. Grill, 6 inches from heat, for about 15 minutes or until the lamb is firm and browned. Serve warm with yogurt sauce.

Burger Sliders

Total Time: 25 Minutes

Prep Time: 15 Minutes

Cook Time: 10 Minutes

Yields: 24 Servings

Ingredients

4 slices bacon

24 small dinner rolls

2 tbsp. Worcestershire sauce

3 pounds lean ground beef

2 garlic cloves, minced

1 finely chopped onion

Salt and pepper

Directions

Cook bacon in a skillet until crisp; drain, discarding all but two tablespoons bacon fat. Sauté onion in bacon fat for about 3 minutes or until translucent. Add garlic and continue cooking for about 30 seconds; transfer to a plate and let cool for a few minutes. When cool enough to handle, crumble bacon.

Combine Worcestershire sauce, onion mixture, bacon, beef, salt and pepper in a large bowl and mix well. Make 24 patties from the mixture and let chill.

Preheat the grill to medium heat and oil once it becomes hot. Cook the burgers, turning hallway through, for about 7 minutes and serve on rolls.

~Omit bacon for a cheaper meal.

Beef Kabobs with Orange Glaze

Total Time: 25 Minutes

Prep Time: 15 Minutes

Cook Time: 10 Minutes

Yields: 8 kabobs

Ingredients

1/4 cup orange juice concentrate, frozen

1/2-pint cherry tomatoes

1 red onion, cut into quarters and layers separated

8 whole mushrooms

1 1/2 pounds boneless sirloin, cubed

4 tbsp. melted unsalted butter

2 tsp. Dijon mustard

1/4 cup soy sauce

Salt and pepper

Directions

Prepare a charcoal fire and let burn to a gray ash or preheat the broiler.

In a small saucepan, stir together butter, mustard, soy sauce and orange juice concentrate over medium-high heat for about 2 minutes or until smooth.

Thread the boneless sirloin onto eight metal skewers, alternating with cherry tomatoes, onions, and whole mushrooms. Brush the soy sauce mixture evenly over the threaded skewers; season with salt and pepper. In a saucepan, bring the remaining glaze to a boil; remove from heat and set aside.

Set the grill or broiling pan 6 inches from the heat source and grill or broil the skewers, turning frequently, for about 6 minutes or until mushrooms and meat are browned and onions charred on edges.

Serve these tasty kabobs warm with glaze on the side.

~Save money by preparing these beef kabobs with sirloin rather than beef tenderloin.

Fajita-Style Quesadillas

These healthy cheesy quesadillas are loaded with crunchy green and red peppers. Plus, it has lime and cilantro to heighten the fresh Spanish flavor without adding extra calories.

Makes: 8 servings

Prep: 20 Minutes

Cook: 8 Minutes

Ingredients

2 thin slices tomato, cut into halves crosswise

1/2 Cup Monterey Jack cheese, shredded

4 6-inch flour tortillas

2 tsp. vegetable oil

1/2 medium onion, halved and thinly sliced

1/2 medium seeded and chopped green or red sweet pepper

Nonstick cooking spray

Cilantro

Lime wedges

Light sour cream

Directions

Cook sweet peppers and onion in large skillet in oil over medium-high heat until the veggies are just tender, for about 5 minutes. Remove skillet from heat.

Lightly coat one side of each tortilla with cooking spray. On the uncoated side of two of the tortillas, divide half of the cheese. Top with 1 tablespoon cilantro, tomato slices, onion mixture, and the remaining cheese. Cover with the remaining tortillas, coated sides up.

Heat a very large skillet or griddle over medium heat. Cook quesadillas for 4 to 5 minutes per side or until cheese melts and tortillas are lightly browned. Cut each quesadilla into 4 wedges. Serve warm and, if desired, with sour cream, additional cilantro and lime wedges.

~You can add chicken or beef strips if desired. However, prepare as a meatless meal for a more budget friendly dish.

Black Bean Burgers

Yield: Serves 4

Cook Time: 20 Minutes

Prep Time: 10 Minutes

Ingredients

2 tbsp. vegetable oil

1/2 cup bread crumbs

1 large egg, lightly beaten

1 15-oz. can rinsed and drained black beans

1 minced clove garlic

1 onion, finely chopped

1 stalk celery, chopped

1 tbsp. cumin

Salt and pepper

Directions

Preheat the oven to 375°F.Prepare a rimmed baking sheet by lining it with foil and coating lightly with oil.

In large skillet, warm oil over medium-high heat. Add onion and celery and cook, stirring frequently, for about 5 minutes or until softened. Add garlic to the skillet and sauté for another 1 minute.

In a large bowl, mash the beans with a potato masher or fork into a thick paste and add the cooked veggies. Stir in bread crumbs, cumin, egg, salt and pepper. Make four patties with your fingers and arrange them on the baking sheet. Bake for about 10 minutes per side or until firm and set. Serve with whole grain buns with sliced red onion, tomato, and lettuce, if desired.

~When buying beans, it is cheaper to buy dried beans and cook them yourself than buying already canned beans.

Carrot Cauliflower Casserole

Yield: 8 Servings

Cook Time: 25 Minutes

Prep Time: 20 Minutes

Ingredients

1/2 Cup bread crumbs

1 1/2 Tablespoons. unsalted butter, melted

3/4 Cup light sour cream

3/4 Cup light mayonnaise

3 cloves garlic, chopped

1 small onion, chopped

1 head cauliflower, cut into florets

1-pound carrots, sliced

Salt and pepper

1 Tablespoons chopped parsley

Directions

Preheat the oven to 425°F. Cook carrots in salted boiling water for about 6 minutes. Add in cauliflower and continue cooking for another 5 minutes and drain. Pour cold water over vegetables to quickly cool.

Use cooking spray to coat a 9×13-inch dish and set aside. Set aside. In a bowl, combine sour cream, mayo, garlic, onion, salt and pepper. Stir in the veggies and transfer to baking dish.

Stir together bread crumbs and butter and sprinkle the mixture over the veggies. Cover the baking dish and bake for about 20 minutes. Sprinkle with parsley and serve.

~This is an easy dish to substitute with whatever vegetables are in season.

Chickpeas and Broccoli

Yield: 4 Servings

Cook Time: 15 Minutes

Prep Time: 10 Minutes

Ingredients

1/3 Cup vegetable or chicken broth

1 can (10.5-oz.) rinsed and drained chickpeas

1 1/2 heads broccoli with stalks, trimmed and chopped

4 cloves garlic, thinly sliced

1 small onion, thinly sliced

2 Tablespoons olive oil

Salt and pepper

1/3 Cup Parmesan shavings

Directions

In skillet, heat oil and sauté garlic and onion. Season with salt and pepper. Sauté until onion is translucent.

Stir in broccoli and continue sautéing for another 3 minutes. Pour in broth. Add chickpeas. Stir and cook, covered, for about 3 minutes or until heated through.

Sprinkle with Parmesan and serve.

~If broccoli isn't in season substitute 2-3 Cups frozen chopped broccoli.

Refried Bean Cups

Yield: 6 Servings

Cook Time: 10 Minutes

Prep Time: 10 Minutes

Ingredients

2 Tablespoons sour cream

1 cup shredded lettuce

6 (6-inch) flour tortillas

1 Cup shredded Cheddar

1 Cup tomato salsa

1 Cup fat-free refried beans

Directions

Preheat the oven to 400°F. Coat a 12-cup muffin tin with cooking spray and set aside.

Place one tortilla in each coated muffin cup and bake for about 8 minutes or until golden.

Divide the beans among the tortilla cups and top with salsa. Sprinkle with shredded cheddar cheese and bake for another 10 minutes or until warmed through.

Place the taco cups on serving plates and sprinkle each serving with lettuce and top with sour cream and more salsa, if desired.

~Save money but making your own refried beans from dried beans.

Orzo Veggie Salad

Yield: 8 Servings

Ingredients

1-pound orzo

1 clove garlic, minced

1 red bell pepper, chopped

1 package (10-oz.) frozen spinach, thawed, squeezed dry and chopped

1 onion, chopped

2 Tablespoons olive oil

Salt and pepper

1/4 Cup grated Parmesan

Directions

Add water to a large pot and bring to a boil; cook orzo, stirring frequently, for about 7 minutes or until tender.'

Meanwhile, in a frying pan, heat one tablespoon oil. Sauté onion and bell pepper, stirring frequently, until tender. Stir in garlic and continue cooking for another minute.

Drain the cooked orzo and return to pot. Stir in the remaining tablespoon oil until well combined. Stir in spinach and onion mixture. Season with salt and pepper and cook over medium-low for about 2 minutes to warm through. Sprinkle with Parmesan cheese and serve!

~Substitute orzo with any small pasta shapes.

Broccoli Casserole

Yield: 10 Servings

Ingredients

1 stick (1/4 lb.) salted butter, cut into pieces

1-pound broccoli, chopped

1 1/2 Cups shredded Cheddar

1 Cup mayonnaise

2 large lightly beaten eggs

1 can (10.75 oz.) cream of mushroom soup

1 sleeve crushed Ritz or saltine crackers

Pepper

Directions

Spray a 9x 13-inch pan with cooking spray and preheat oven to 350°F.

Cook broccoli until crisp-tender, drain, and rinse with cold water.

In a saucepan or microwave safe dish, add butter. Once butter melts stir in eggs, soup, cheese, mayonnaise, and pepper. Stir to combine and stirring, for a few minutes or until melted and mixed.

Add broccoli into pan and pour sauce over top of broccoli. Sprinkle with crushed crackers and bake for 20-30 minutes.

~If the budget allows, add in 1 Cup chopped cooked chicken. Sometimes buying Rotisserie chicken is cheaper than buying raw chicken breasts and the shredded chicken works well in this recipe.

Cheesy Bread Bake

Yield: 4 Servings

Ingredients

1 tsp. Worcestershire sauce

1 1/2 Cups milk

3 large eggs

4 slices French bread or sandwich bread

8 ounces shredded Cheddar cheese,

1 teaspoon dried onions or onion powder

pinch of black pepper

pinch of salt

Directions

Coat a small 8x8 casserole dish with butter or cooking spray. Lay bread on the bottom of the dish to form a crust.

In a bowl, beat together milk, eggs, Worcestershire sauce, onion powder, salt and pepper until well blended. Stir in cheese. Pour mixture over the bread. Let sit for 15-30 minutes.

Preheat your oven to 375°F.

Place in oven and bake until the top is golden browned, about 20-30 minutes.

~All the ingredients in this recipe are common, cheap items you should have stocked in your kitchen.

Texas Hash

Cooking Time: 1 hour

Ingredients

1-pound ground beef

1 Tablespoon chili powder

2 medium size tomatoes, diced

1 small green pepper, diced

1 small onion, diced

1/2 Cup water

1/2 Cup uncooked instant rice

1/8 tsp. pepper

1 tsp. salt

Directions:

Preheat the oven to 350°F.

Brown the ground beef with green pepper, onion and season with chili powder. Add in chopped tomatoes. Cook several minutes until tomatoes soften. Drain.

Stir rice and water together with the meat mixture into a small casserole dish and combine well.

Bake, covered, for at least 60 minutes.

Sprinkle the top with shredded cheese if desired.

~I can buy chopped vegetables like onion and green peppers in the freezer section which often is cheaper than fresh vegetables.

Spicy Buffalo Chicken Tenders
Ingredients

Breaded chicken tenders

1/2 Cup Hot Sauce

1/4 teaspoon cayenne pepper

1/4 teaspoon garlic powder

1/4 teaspoon onion powder

4 Tablespoons butter or margarine

Blue cheese salad dressing, for dipping

Directions:

Cook chicken tenders according to package direction. Meanwhile, mix the remaining ingredients in a saucepan and heat until butter is melted, for about 2 minutes.

Place each chicken into the hot sauce mixture and coat well.

Serve the tenders immediately with Bleu cheese dressing.

~If it is cheaper for you, buy fresh chicken, cut in cubes and make your own chicken tenders

Beefy Barbecue Sandwich

Cooking Time: 8 hours

Yields: 12 Servings

Ingredients

3 pounds boneless beef chuck roast

1 small onion, chopped

12 hamburger rolls

2 tsp. brown sugar

1 Tablespoon yellow mustard

1 Tablespoon Worcestershire sauce

1 sweet red or green pepper, chopped finely

2 Cups barbecue sauce

Directions

Cut the beef roast into four portions and place them in a slow cooker.

Combine brown sugar, mustard, barbecue sauce, onion, and green pepper, in a large bowl; pour over the roast. Cover the pot and cook on low until meat is tender, for about 7 hours.

Shred meat into thin pieces; return to pot and stir gently. Cover and continue cooking for about 30 more minutes. Top each roll with beef and more sauce, if desired.

Spaghetti Pizza Pie

Make this simple pasta pie for a quick and budget friendly weeknight dinner.

Total Time: 55 Minutes

Prep Time: 15 Minutes

Cook Time: 30 Minutes

Cool: 10 Minutes

Yield: 6 Servings

Ingredients

1/2 Cup milk

8 large eggs

8 ounces uncooked spaghetti

2 Tablespoons butter, cut into small pieces

1/4 Cup Parmesan cheese, finely shredded

1/4 Cup mozzarella cheese, shredded

1/3 Cup diced ham or pepperoni

1/4 tsp. freshly ground pepper

Directions

Preheat the oven to 400°F. Spray an 8x8 inch casserole dish with cooking spray. Set aside.

Cook spaghetti according to package instructions. Drain cooked pasta, rinse with cold water and drain again.

In a bowl, blend together ham, milk, eggs, 3 tablespoon Parmesan, mozzarella, and pepper. Stir in cooked spaghetti and combine until well coated. Spread the mixture into a dish and add small pieces of butter over the top. Sprinkle with the remaining Parmesan cheese and mozzarella cheese. Bake for about 30 minutes. Cool slightly before cutting.

Easy Guacamole Recipe

Total:20 Minutes

Servings: 4

Ingredients

Extra virgin olive oil

1 ripe peeled avocado

1/2 small jalapeño pepper

1garlic clove

1/8 teaspoon salt

1 Tablespoon fresh lime juice

1 1/2 Tablespoons red onion, coarsely chopped

1 Tablespoon cilantro leaves

Directions

Blend jalapeno pepper, extra virgin olive oil, garlic clove, salt, lime juice, and red onion in food processor until finely chopped. Add avocado and continue processing until very smooth. Sprinkle with cilantro and refrigerate before serving.

~A great time to buy avocadoes is during spring to fall, when they are in season.

FRUGAL LUNCH RECIPES

Chicken and Broccoli Curry

Yield: 4 Servings

Cook Time: 20 Minutes

Prep Time: 10 Minutes

Ingredients

1 1/2 pounds chicken breast, cubes

1 (10 oz.) box broccoli florets, frozen, thawed

1 (14 oz.) can chicken broth~

1 1/2 tsp. curry powder

1 large onion, coarsely chopped

2 Tablespoons vegetable oil

1/4 Cup cornstarch

1/2 tsp. pepper

3/4 tsp. kosher salt

1/2 Cup sour cream

Directions

In a large bowl, stir together cornstarch, curry powder, pepper and salt. Toss in chicken cubes and toss to coat.

In a skillet, heat 2 Tablespoons oil and sauté onion. Cook until onion softens. Add in chicken cubes and cook until chicken is lightly browned.

Add in broth and let simmer on medium heat about 5-10 minutes. Add in broccoli. Cook until broccoli is tender. Take off heat and stir in sour cream.

~It is often cheaper to buy bouillon cubes and make your own broth with water, then buying canned or boxed broth. Do whatever's cheaper for you in this recipe.

Walnuts and Apples Green Salad

Yield: Serves 8

Cook Time: 8 Minutes

Prep Time: 10 Minutes

Ingredients

1/2 Cup walnut pieces

8 Cups mixed salad greens

1/3 Cup olive oil

2 cored and halved Granny Smith apples, chopped into thin slices

1 tsp. sugar

1 Tablespoon Dijon mustard

1/4 Cup white wine vinegar

Salt and pepper

Directions

Toast walnuts in 350-degree oven for 5-8 minutes.

Prepare dressing in a small jar by adding vinegar, sugar, mustard, oil, salt and pepper. Place lid on jar and shake to combine well.

In serving bowl, toss together salad greens, cooled walnuts and chopped apples. Drizzle with dressing before serving.

~ Walnuts can be bought in bulk and frozen in a tight container.

Creamy Tomato Soup

Yield: 8 Servings

Cook Time: 15 Minutes

Prep Time: 10 Minutes

Ingredients

2 Tablespoons butter

1/2 Cup heavy cream

1 1/2 Cups chicken broth

1 28-oz. can crushed tomatoes, with juice

2 Tablespoons. flour

1 clove garlic, chopped

1 onion, chopped

Salt and pepper

Directions

In a large saucepan, heat butter over medium heat. Sauté onion for about 5 minutes or until softened. Add garlic and let cook for another 1 minute. Whisk in flour until well combined, making a roux.

Whisk in broth until lumps dissolve. Add in tomatoes with juice to the pan and bring soup to a boil. Whisk the mixture for about 3 minutes while soup thickens.

Pour half the soup into a blender and process until smooth. Pour into serving bowl and puree other half of soup. Add to serving bowl and stir in cream.   Season with salt and pepper.

~Create your heart warming and healthy version of the tomato soup that is cheaper than the can you would purchase at the store.

Corn Black Bean Salad

Yield: Serves 8

Cook Time: 20 Minutes

Prep Time: 20 Minutes

Ingredients

2 Tablespoons plus 1/3 Cup olive oil

2 teaspoons. Dijon mustard

3 Tablespoons rice wine vinegar

3 tomatoes cored, seeded and chopped

2 15 oz cans black beans, drained and rinsed

1/4 Cup chopped parsley or cilantro

2 Cups corn kernels

1 onion, chopped

Salt and pepper

Directions

In skillet heat 2 Tablespoons oil and sauté onion, for about 2-3 minutes or until tender. Add in corn kernels. Combine the corn mixture, tomatoes, beans, and parsley in a large bowl.

In a separate bowl or container, combine mustard, vinegar, salt and pepper and whisk to dissolve salt and combine the ingredients well. Add in 1/3 cup oil, combine well.

Pour dressing over corn mixture and season with salt and pepper.

Budget Vegan Lentil Soup

Total Time: 40 Minutes

Prep Time: 10 Minutes

Cook Time: 30 Minutes

Ingredients:

Serves: 10

5 -6 new potatoes, chopped

2 Cups red lentils

5 garlic cloves, diced

1 vegetable bouillon cube

10 Cups water

2 -3 Tablespoons olive oil

1 onion, diced

2 carrots, sliced

salt and pepper

Directions

In a large pan, heat oil. Sauté garlic and onions for a few minutes or until onion are soft.

Dissolve bouillon cube in one cup of water. Pour into large pan. Add potatoes, lentils, carrots, salt, pepper, and the remaining water to the pan. Stir well to combine. Cook the mixture for 10-15 minutes or until potatoes are tender.

Cucumber Salad

Yield: Serves 8

Prep Time: 10 Minutes

Ingredients

2 Tablespoons chopped fresh dill or 1 teaspoon dried dill

2 Tablespoons olive oil

3 Tablespoons rice wine vinegar

1 red onion, cut into thin slices

3 cucumbers, cut in thin slices

Salt and pepper

Directions

Add cucumbers and sliced onions to a serving bowl. In a jar blend together oil, vinegar, dill and a pinch of salt and pepper. Shake to combine well.

Pour dressing over cucumbers. Season with more salt and pepper if needed.

~Cucumbers are an easy budget friendly addition to dinner.

~A tasty addition is to add 1-2 fresh tomatoes, chopped finely.

Texas Stew

Yield: 8 Servings

Cook Time: 5 Hours

Prep Time: 15 Minutes

Ingredients

1/4 Cup all-purpose flour

2 pounds beef tips, cubed

1/2 Cup water

1 package (10-oz.) frozen whole-kernel corn

1 jar (8-oz.) taco sauce (mild)

1 can (10.5 oz.) beef broth, undiluted

1 can (14.5 oz.) Mexican-style stewed tomatoes

1/2 tsp. ground cumin

2 garlic cloves, pressed

1 onion, cut small wedges

3 carrots, cut into small pieces

1/2 tsp. salt

Directions

In a 5-quart slow cooker, combine corn, taco sauce, broth, tomatoes, beef, cumin, garlic, onion, carrots, and salt. Cook, covered, on high heat for about 4 hours or until the meat is softened.

One hour before serving, in a bowl, combine flour and water. Stir into the meat mixture; and continue to cook 1 hour.

Crunchy Broccoli Slaw

Yield: 8 Servings

Cook Time: 10 Minutes

Prep Time: 25 Minutes

Ingredients

1 large head broccoli

8 slices bacon

2 Tablespoons honey

3 Tablespoons white balsamic vinegar

1/3 Cup mayonnaise

1/3 Cup raisins or Craisins

1 small red onion, minced (1/2 cup), optional

Salt and pepper

Directions

In a large griddle or skillet, cook bacon over medium-high heat for about 10 minutes or until crisp and browned. Crumble the cooked bacon into ½-ich pieces and set aside.

Separate the broccoli florets from the stems and chop them into small pieces. Place broccoli into a salad bowl and toss with raisins and minced onion.

Blend together vinegar and mayonnaise in a small bowl until smooth. Whisk in honey, salt and pepper and pour the dressing over the broccoli mixture. Toss to coat evenly; crumble the bacon over broccoli salad and enjoy!

~If you have chopped almonds or sunflower seeds on hand this makes a nice addition to this salad.

Potato Soup

Yield: Serves 6

Cook Time: 30 Minutes

Prep Time: 10 Minutes

Ingredients

4 slices bacon

4 baking potatoes

4 ounces sour cream

4 ounces shredded Monterey Jack

4 Cups milk

1/3 Cup all-purpose flour

4 Tablespoons butter

2 Tablespoons chopped scallions or chives~

Salt and pepper

Directions

Bake potatoes in the oven and allow to cool. If you're in a hurry, microwave potatoes for 15 minutes. Mash potatoes.

Cook bacon in a skillet until crisp, cool and crumble.

In a soup pan, melt butter over medium heat. Whisk in flour making a roux. Whisk in milk slowly and cook, whisking for about 6 minutes or until thickened.

Add in mashed potatoes, cheese and season with a pinch of salt and pepper. Cook the mixture, stirring constantly, until the cheese is melted and the soup is heated through. Blend in sour cream before serving. Add additional salt and pepper if needed. Sprinkle each serving with chives and bacon.

~Growing a small herb garden is a great frugal way to season your meals!

~If you have leftover mashed potatoes from previous dinners, this is a great way to use those up!

Red Potato Salad

Yield: 8 Servings

Cook Time: 30 Minutes

Prep Time: 15 Minutes

Cool: 25 Minutes

Ingredients

3 pounds red potatoes

Zest of 1 lemon

1 Cup mayonnaise

2 tsp. Dijon mustard

2 Tablespoons. minced red onion

2 stalks celery, minced

1/4 Cup apple cider vinegar

1 1-oz. packet vegetable soup mix

pinch of pepper

1 Tablespoon parsley, dried

Directions

In large pot, add potatoes and cover with water and bring to a boil. Cook until tender. Drain and set aside.

Cut potatoes into bite size pieces and place in a serving bowl. In separate bowl, add vinegar, soup mix and pepper and toss to mix well. Pour over cooked potatoes. Cover with plastic wrap and chill in the refrigerator for an hour.

Before serving stir in lemon zest, parsley, mayonnaise, mustard, onion, and chopped celery. Toss to coat well. Season with salt and pepper if desired.

Cream of Celery Soup
Ingredients

2 Tablespoons olive oil

1/2 Cup cream

1-quart vegetable stock

1 Tablespoon dried parsley

1 garlic clove, chopped

1 large onion, chopped

1 head celery, sliced

Pinch nutmeg

Directions

Add onion, celery and garlic in a pan with olive oil and cook over low for about 15 minutes or until celery softens. Add in stock and parsley; season with pepper and bring the mixture to a boil and simmer for about 10 minutes. Pour soup into blender or using a hand blender puree soup. Stir in cream and serve.

~You can usually always find celery cheap year-round so it makes a budget friendly and healthy addition to meals.

Butter Parsley Noodles

Yield: 8 Servings

Cook Time: 10 Minutes

Prep Time: 10 Minutes

Ingredients

3 Tablespoons butter

1 package (12-oz.) medium egg noodles

1 onion, chopped

2 Tablespoons dried parsley

Salt

Ground black pepper

Directions

Cook noodles according to package directions. In saucepan, melt butter and in onion and sauté until tender.

Drain the noodles and reserve about 1/4 cup cooking liquid. Return the cooked noodles to pot; stir in onion-butter mixture and season with parsley, salt and pepper. Add the reserved cooking liquid a tablespoon at a time, if the noodles appear dry. Serve hot.

~A simple recipe with cheap food staples you usually have stocked in your kitchen.

Creamy Risotto

Yield: 6 Servings

Ingredients

1/3 Cup shredded Parmesan

1-pound orzo

1 Tablespoon parsley

1 teaspoon dried mixed herbs or thyme

1 small finely chopped onion

1 Tablespoon butter

Black pepper

1 Cup milk

1 Cup cream of mushroom soup

Directions

Boil salted water and add orzo. Follow package directions to cook until al dente; drain in a colander.

In a small pan, melt butter and add in seasonings and onion.

Whisk in milk and soup. Stir in cooked orzo, Top each serving with Parmesan cheese.

~If you prefer to use fresh herbs, you can substitute for the dried in this recipe. Dried herbs are usually cheaper than fresh store bought. If you grow your own it is even cheaper!

Tuna-and-Macaroni Salad

Yield: Serves 8

Cook Time: 7 Minutes

Prep Time: 15 Minutes

Ingredients

1 Tablespoon cider vinegar, plus 1 tsp.

1-pound elbow macaroni

1/4 Cup plain low-fat yogurt

1/2 Cup reduced-fat mayonnaise, plus 2 tbsp.

1 12-oz. can tuna in water, drained

1 carrot, grated

1/2 Cup fresh parsley, finely chopped

1/2 Cup red onion, finely diced

3 ribs finely chopped celery

Salt

Ground black pepper

Directions

Cook macaroni according to package directions until tender. Drain and rinse with cold water. Set aside.

In a serving bowl, add together tuna, carrot, parsley, onion, and celery. Add macaroni and toss to mix well. In separate bowl or measuring cup, whisk vinegar, yogurt, and mayonnaise. Season with salt and pepper and whisk to combine well. Pour the mixture over pasta and toss to coat well. Cover and place in the refrigerator until ready to serve.

~Tuna is a cheap staple to stock up on when it goes on sale. You can use it in casseroles, salads, sandwiches, quesadillas, etc.

Clean out the Cupboard Veggie Soup

Total Time: 20 Minutes

Prep Time: 0 Minutes

Cook Time: 20 Minutes

Servings: 6

Ingredients:

1 lb small shell pasta or other pasta you have on hand

1 (10 1/2-ounce) can tomato soup

1 can corn

1 can green beans

1 1/2 Cups water

1/2 tsp. ground pepper

2 Tablespoons garlic salt

2 Tablespoons basil

Directions

in a large pan, combine tomato soup, corn, water, and green beans. Add basil, salt and pepper and bring to a rolling boil. Add shell pasta and cook the mixture for about 19 minutes or until pasta is al dente.

~Buying canned vegetables on sale can be cheaper sometimes then buying fresh produce. Stock up when the sales are on.

Chicken and Rice

Servings: 4

Ingredients

1 Cup uncooked rice

4 pieces chicken thighs

1/2 tsp. Turmeric

2-inch piece ginger, minced

2 garlic cloves, minced

2 leek or onions, chopped finely

5 Cups water

Directions

In a large pan, sauté leeks, ginger and garlic several minutes. Add in chicken thighs. Season with turmeric. Add rice and stir to coat.

Add 5 cups of water lower the heat and simmer for half an hour.

Divide into serving bowls and top with a drizzle of soy sauce, if desired.

Chicken Fried Rice

Total Time: 22 Minutes

Prep Time: 7 Minutes

Cook Time: 15 Minutes

Yield: 4 Servings

Ingredients

3 eggs

1-2 Cups chopped chicken breast or shredded Rotisserie chicken

4 Cups cooked white rice

2 Tablespoons soy sauce

1/2 package (10-oz.) frozen mixed vegetables, thawed

3/4 Cup chopped onion

1/4 Cup vegetable oil

2 tsp. sesame oil

Kosher salt

Black pepper

Directions

Marinade chicken in sesame oil and soy sauce for 30 minutes. Heat frying pan and add 1 Tablespoon oil, sauté onion until tender. Add in chicken and cook until cooked through. Stir in vegetables and cooked rice. Stir to combine well

Make a well in the mixture and add the eggs inside the hole. Scramble until just soft. Stir eggs into rice. Season with salt and pepper, if needed.

~I like to buy Rotisserie chicken. Often it is cheaper than buying a roast chicken and roasting it myself and I find the shredded chicken can be used for 2 meals.

Chicken, Tomato, and Avocado Sandwich

Total Time: 5 minutes

Active Time: 5 minutes

Serving Size: 1 sandwich

Ingredients

2 slices tomato

3 ounces cooked chicken breast, boneless, skinless, sliced

1/4 ripe avocado

2 slices multigrain bread, toasted

Directions

Mash avocado and spread on toasted bread slice. Top with cooked chicken and slices of tomato. Add another slice of bread to the top for a sandwich.

~Another meal that would be could using Rotisserie chicken.

Cobb Egg Salad

Total Time: 15 minutes

Active Time: 15 minutes

Makes: 4 servings

Ingredients

1/4 Cup cheese crumbles, whatever flavor you like or is on sale

2 slices cooked and crumbled bacon

1 ripe avocado, cubed

8 hard-boiled eggs

3 Tablespoons mayonnaise

3 Tablespoons Greek or nonfat plain yogurt

1/8 tsp. salt

1/4 tsp. ground pepper

Directions

Blend together yogurt, salt, pepper, and mayonnaise. Stir until well combined. Mash hard boiled eggs into the yogurt mixture. Stir in cheese cubes, bacon and avocado.

Cream of Broccoli Soup

This soup will surprise you just how broccoli can be delicious without butter, stock, or onion. The secret to this broccoli soup is being generous with pepper and salt and not adding too much water.

Servings: 1

Yields: 8 servings

Ingredients

2 heads broccoli, chopped

3 cloves garlic, peeled, chopped

1 large onion, chopped

1 tbsp. olive oil

4 Cups vegetable broth

2 peeled and chopped potatoes

1 teaspoon thyme

Pinch salt

Pinch pepper

Directions

Sauté onion and garlic with oil in a soup pan until tender. Stir in broccoli, broth, and chopped potatoes and bring the mixture to a gentle boil. Lower the heat to low and simmer for about 15-20 minutes or until potatoes are tender.

Transfer the mixture to a blender and puree until smooth. Season with salt, thyme and pepper.

~If broccoli isn't in season, use 2 -10 oz. bags of frozen broccoli